PURLIE
and her friends
18 inch Knitted DOLLS and Three Knitted Outfits

By Betty Lampen
and Karen Richardson

Contents

Instructions and Materials .... Inside Front Cover

PURLIE, The Doll..2

PURLIE the doll pattern 3-4

Putting PURLIE Together...5

Party Dress 6-7

Bloomers 8

Purse and Party Shoes 9

Peasant Costume 10

Peasant Costume cont., Apron, Slip & Hat 10-11

Stockings and Clogs..12

Cardigan 13-14

Pants...14

Easy Undies and Sneakers 15

Hair Styles and Knitting Tips 16

© 2000 Betty Lampen 2930 Jackson St. San Francisco, Calif. 94115-1007

PURLIE

PURLIE The 18" Doll
Pattern for this doll is the same as for "STITCHES" Book 1.
ALL STOCKINETTE
Size 7 & 4 needles. Tapestry needle.
3 oz 4 ply worsted yarn skin color & 1 or 2 oz hair color.
6 oz of polyester fiber for stuffing.

Body With skin color yarn, size 7 needles. Cast on 44 sts, knit 44 rows 7-1/2".
Shoulders Knit 6 sts *(right half of back neck)*. With a tapestry needle put next 10 sts on a separate piece of yarn, *(see page 6 for shoulder directions)*, knit 12 sts (front neck), put 10 sts on separate piece of yarn *(for other shoulder)*, knit 6 sts *(left half of back)* (24 sts on needle).

Neck Change to size 4 needles. Knit 2 rows.
Next row, knit 1, increase 1, across row (47 sts).
Important – See INCREASING *directions on page 5*.
Change to size 7 needles. Knit across and increase 1 st at beg. of every row for 3 rows. (50 sts). *Mark row for neck weave, see page 5*.
Knit 2 more rows.

Now comes the decision whether to continue knitting scalp in skin color yarn (to add hair later) **OR** as with Purlie, to follow the pattern below. Either way, except for the change of yarn, the basic pattern (of 14 rows plain, 6 rows decrease) is the same.

Face & Hair *Knit face and hair together:*
Row 1. Knit 16 sts hair, 18 sts face, 16 sts hair.
Row 2. Purl back in pattern.
Row 3. Knit 17 sts hair, 16 sts face, 17 sts hair.
Row 4. Purl back in pattern.
Row 5. Purl 18 sts hair, 14 sts face, 18 sts hair.
Row 6. Purl back in pattern.
Row 7. Knit 19 sts hair, 12 sts face, 19 sts hair.
Row 8. Purl back in pattern.
Row 9. Knit 20 sts hair, 10 sts face, 20 sts hair.
Row 10. Purl back in pattern.
Row 11, 12, 13, 14. Knit all hair color yarn.

Top of Head – Start decrease
Row 15. Knit 3 sts, knit 2 sts together across row (40 sts).
Row 16. Knit. Row 17. Knit 2 sts tog., knit 2 sts across row (30 sts).
Row 18. Knit. Row 19. Knit 2 sts tog. knit 2 sts. across row (22 sts).
Row 20. Knit. Row 21. Knit 2 sts tog. across row (11 sts).
Row 22. Knit back.
Row 23. With size 4 needle knit 3 sts, knit 2 sts tog. across row. (9 sts.).
With tapestry needle thread yarn through last 9 sts.
Pull yarn tight, so no hole is left. Tuck yarn into head.

PURLIE – *continued*

Legs Size 7 needles.
Starting at foot.
Top of Foot Cast on 30 sts.
Knit 1 row. Next row knit 6 sts, bind off 6 sts, knit 6 sts, bind off 6 sts, knit last 6 sts. *(18 sts left on needle)*. With separate yarn, knit center 6 sts *(for top of foot)*. Knit 6 rows. Cut yarn.
Join all 18 sts.
Ankle Decrease 1 st at beg. and end of row. (16 sts)
Leg Knit and increase 1 st every 8th row (3 times) to 19 sts.
Knit 6-1/2" *(measure from back heel of cast on)*. Bind off.
Sole Pick up 5 sts at center front of foot (at cast on edge).
Knit 11 rows. Bind off.
See page 5 for finish.

Arms Starting at hand end cast on 14 sts. Knit 32 rows.
For shoulder flap decrease 1 st at beg. of every row until 6 sts are on needle (7" from cast on). Bind off.

* * * * * * * * * * * * *

CURLS: Size G crochet hook: To make one curl, leave 3" of yarn and chain 24 sts, turn, crochet 2 sts in each chain stitch. *Work will curl.* Leave 3" of yarn at end and cut yarn . With those 3 inches of yarn at beg. and end of each curl, tie knot **inside the head of Purlie before stuffing .**

For single row of curls around first row of hair color, crochet 16 curls and knot on inside of head.

To cover the whole head, fifty curls will be needed.
THAT is a real labor of love!
Longer curls will make dreadlocks.
Straight fringe can be added (instead of curls) over the face.

For more hair styles see page 16.

Putting PURLIE Together

Shoulders Put 10 bound off (or held) sts on 2 double pointed needles. Put 5 of those sts on one double pointed needle. Put the other 5 sts on 2nd double pointed needle. Fold needles and stitches to weave (or sew) sts together to make a shoulder 5 sts wide. Repeat 'operation' on other shoulder with other 10 sts.

Seam sewing. To join knitting, use flat seam stitch. See page 16 for directions. Stitch seams with same colored yarn as knitting (hair color for hair and skin color yarn for body).

Increasing – Pick up new stitch from BACK of next stitch ONE ROW DOWN to make a 'not too obvious' increase, especially for the neck of the doll.

Knot and Stuff Sew up body leaving one opening. Turn doll inside out. Knot and/or stitch yarns together firmly into knitting. For Purlie only, knot curl ends inside head. Turn right side out. With polyester fiber, stuff body. Stuff the head very firm. Sew arm and leg seams, leave opening at bottom of each part. Turn inside out, knot and/or stitch yarn inside limbs. Check and darn any possible unintential holes. Stitch all pieces closed. A weaving st (see page 16) at bottom of body gives a smooth finish. HOW YOU STUFF YOUR DOLL IS HOW HER CLOTHES WILL FIT!

Neck & Wrists With skin color yarn weave single strand on increase row of neck. Pull tight. Knot at center back of doll and tuck yarn ends into stuffing. A second strand of weaving can also be stitched below the first row of weaving if a longer neck is desired. Weave same way on wrists and ankles about 1-1/2" from cast on.

Legs Sew flat seams on sides of feet and back of legs. Stuff. Sew leg closed across top of leg, feet forward. Stitch legs firmly to front of the body on the 5th row above cast on row. Make sure feet face forward. Allow for sitting position and legs that swing back and forth.

Arms Sew seams and stuff. Stitch top 6 sts (of arm flap) on the 2nd row of shoulder fold on body. Stitch arm carefully down both sides on top of knitted body for about 1-1/2". Add a bit more stuffing while stitching to increase shoulder width.

Hand For a good hand finish, before sewing up or stuffing, unravel the cast on sts. With double pointed needles put 3 sts on one needle, 7 sts on next needle and 4 sts on 3rd needle. Weave 7 center sts to the 3 and 4 sts (like the toe of a sock).

Face With a tapestry needle stitch a bit of eye color (blue, green, gray or brown), a bit of red for the lips, perhaps a bit of skin color for the nose. To sew features on face so that they do not come out, with an extra long needle, bring yarn from back of head through stuffing to face, stitch desired feature and bring yarn back through the head to the same place. Knot both ends and bury yarn back into stuffing.

Party Dress

Stockinette. Size 3 & 6 needles. E Crochet hook. 3 oz sport yarn, pink. A bit of white yarn. 4 snaps. Dress knit in one piece (except sleeves).

Starting at bottom of skirt

With Size 3 needle, cast on 130 sts.
Rib K1, P1 3 rows.
Change to size 6 needles.
Stockinette. (4-1/2" from cast on).
Starting on a knit row cast on 2 sts *(left side, center back)*. (132 sts)
Knit those 2 sts in garter st for the rest of the dress, for snaps.
A marker would be helpful).
Knit 4 rows, end with purl row and the 2 garter sts.

PURLIE
Hair page 4

Waist Row 1 *First decrease* Knit 2 sts garter st, knit 2 sts tog. knit 2 st, across row. (97 sts & 2 garter sts, 99 sts). Row 2 Purl 1 row. Row 3 *Second decrease*. Knit 2 garter sts, knit 1 st, knit 2 sts tog. across row (66 sts & 2 garter sts, 68 sts). Knit 12 rows.

Underarm Knit 1 row and divide sts for underarm.
Left Back: 13 sts plus 2 garter sts (15 sts). Bind off 7 sts (underarm).
Front: 26 sts. Bind off 7 sts (underarm). **Right Back:** 13 sts.

Left Back 13 sts and 2 garter sts, knit 12 rows.
Shoulder Hold 8 st & 2 garter st (for neck rib). Knit 5 sts 6 rows. Bind off.

Front Knit 26 sts, 12 rows. **Shoulders** Knit 9 sts, decrease 1 st at neck edge every other row until 5 sts are left. Knit 2 more rows (10 rows). Hold center 8 sts (for neck rib). Knit last 9 sts. Decrease 1 sts at neck edge until 5 sts are left. Knit 2 more rows. Bind off.

Right Back Knit 13 sts 12 rows.
Shoulder Knit 5 sts 6 rows. Bind off. Hold 8 sts (for neck rib).

Neck With Size 3 needles pick up 42 and 2 garter sts (44 sts) as follows: 8 sts for right side of back, 9 sts shoulder, 8 sts front, 9 sts shoulder, 8 sts & 2 garter sts left side of back.
Rib K1, P1 42 sts & 2 garter sts 3 rows. Bind off in ribbing.

Party Dress – *continued*

Two kinds of sleeves. Plain (in photo) and puffed (not shown).

1. Sleeves With size 3 needles cast on 26 sts. Rib K 1, P 1, 3 rows.
Change to size 6 needles.
Stockinette. Knit 1 st, increase 1 st across row (38 sts).
Knit 3".
Underarm Bind off 3 sts at beg. of row and 4 sts at beg. of next row. (31 sts). Dec 1 st at beg. and end of every knit row until 27 sts are left. Bind off 2 sts at beg of next 2 rows. (19 sts) Knit 2 sts together across last row, ending with knit 1 st (10 sts). Bind off.

2. Sleeves – puffed (not shown). With size 3 needles. Cast on 26 sts.
Rib K 1, P 1 3 rows.
Change to size 6 needles. Stockinette. First row Knit 1 st, increase 1 st across row (51 sts). Knit 3".
Underarm Bind off 3 sts at beg of row and 4 sts at beg of next row (44 sts).
Knit and decrease 1 st both ends every row until there are 28 sts on the needle.
Knit 2 sts tog. across row (14 sts). Bind off.

Finish With tapestry needle, sew up back of skirt with a flat stitch to 2 st garter stitch addition. With pink yarn crochet one single crochet row up back opening on side without garter st edge. Sew 4 snaps garter st edge and crochet row on back of dress. Sew sleeves onto dress (start by lining up and sewing underarm sts together). Tuck in all loose threads. With tapestry needle and white yarn, Duplicate Stitch (see page 16) pattern below for finishing touch on skirt of the dress.

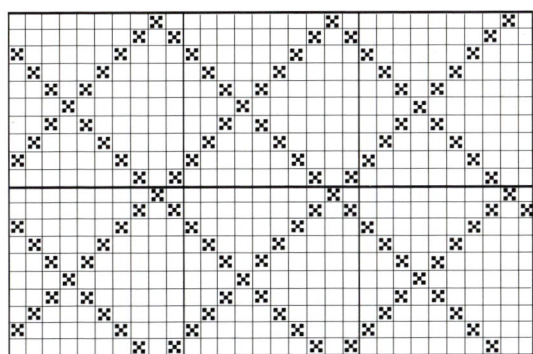

DUPLICATE STITCH DESIGN FOR PARTY DRESS SKIRT

Party Dress Bloomers

2 oz   Pink Sport Yarn   Size 3 & 6 needles.
Stockinette   E crochet hook.

BLOOMERS: RIGHT SIDE
Size 3 needles cast on 40 sts. Knit 1 row. Row 2. Knit 2 sts together *, yarn over, k 2 sts tog. * across row *(for waist tie)*. Change to size 6 needles. Knit <u>one</u> row.
To make the bloomers higher in the back, knit as follows:
* Knit 6 sts, turn, slip 1 st, k 5 sts. Turn, k 12 sts , turn, slip 1 st, k 11 sts. Turn, k 18 sts, turn, slip 1 st, k 17 sts. Turn, knit 40 sts.
Knit 1 st., increase 1 st at the beg. of every row to 60 sts. (see Note below).
(Crotch). Knit 1 row.
Leg   Knit 1 st, decrease 1 st at the beg. of every row for 8 rows (52 sts). Change to size 3 needles: *K 2 sts tog., yarn over * across row (for leg tie). Knit 3 rows, garter stitch. Bind off .

BLOOMERS: LEFT SIDE
Size 3 needles cast on 40 sts. K 1 row. K 2 sts tog. yarn over, across row. Change to size 6 needles. Knit <u>two </u>rows. Continue same pattern as right side from *Knit 6 sts, turn, etc. **STOP** and make sure that those rows are on the correct (opposite) side of the back where both pieces will be joined.

Finish   With flat stitch *(see page 16)*. Join 2 pieces from cast on to crotch both sides. *(Back seam is longer than front)*. Sew both leg seams from crotch to bottom of bloomers.

Ties   With E crochet hook and pink yarn, chain one strip 20" long for waist band. Chain 2 more strips 18" long for leg ties. Weave crochet strips through holes around waist and legs. Finish with bows.

Note: To **increase** for a neat hidden st, pick up new stitch <u>from the back</u> of the next knit stitch <u>one row down</u>. To increase or decrease sts, for both knitting and purling, knit second st in from edge. (i.e. Knit one stitch, increase one stitch **or** knit one stitch, decrease one stitch).

Purlie's Party Dress Purse

Size 1 and 3 needles. E crochet hook.
1 oz pink and white sport yarn. 1 oz Fingering yarn.

        Starting at top of purse with size 3 needles and pink yarn,
Cast on 40 sts. Change to Size 1 and white fingering yarn.
Knit 6 rows in seed st. *See directions below.**
Change to size 3 needles and pink yarn.
Knit 3-1/2" from cast on.
Start decrease. Row 1: Knit 3 sts, k 2 sts tog. across row (32 sts).
Row 2: K 2 sts, K 2 sts tog. across row (24 sts). Row 3: K 1 st, K 2
sts tog. across row (16 sts). Row 4: K 2 sts tog. across row. (8 sts).
With tapestry needle catch 8 sts. Gather and stitch down. Sew seam.
Crochet two 8" chains. Thread both chains through holes
(under seed st. rows). Pull so there are two handles on opposite
sides of bag. Knot chain ends. Tuck in all yarns.

Finish   Cut cardboard in a circle 2-1/4" across. Stitch inside bottom of bag.

* **Seed Stitch** First row: knit 1, purl 1. Second row: knit the purl stitch and purl the knit stitch. Repeat those 2 rows for seed stitch.

****

PURLIE'S PARTY DRESS SHOES 'n SOCKS   (DIFFICULT)

Party Shoes 'n Socks (2)   Knit in one piece.
        Size 5 needles. Sport yarn. Grey sole. Black shoe. White sock.
Garter stitch sole and shoe. Stockinette sock.

Sole   Grey yarn. Cast on 20 sts. <u>Row 1</u>: Knit <u>Row 2</u>: Knit 2 sts, inc 1 st, knit 1 st, inc 1 st, knit 6 st, (inc 1 st, knit 1 st) 3 times, inc 1 st, knit 5 sts, inc 1 st, knit 1 st, inc 1 st , knit 2 sts, (28 sts on needle).
<u>Row 3</u>: Knit 10 sts. inc 1 st, knit 3 sts, inc 1 st, knit 2 sts, inc 1 st, knit 3 sts, inc 1 st, knit 10 sts (32 sts on needle). Cut yarn.
Always leave enough yarn to sew item together.

Shoe   Change to black yarn. <u>Rows 4 thru 10:</u> Knit every row [7 rows].

Shoe and Sock <u>Row 11</u>: Black yarn knit 12 sts, k 2 black sts tog. white yarn purl 4 sts *(Keep white center sts in stockinette – knit side out)*. With separate ball of black yarn k 2 black sts tog, knit 12 black sts [30 sts]
<u>Row 12</u>: Knit 10 black sts, k 2 black sts tog, k 6 white sts, k 2 black st tog, knit 10 black sts. <u>Row 13</u>: Knit 9 black sts, k 2 black sts tog, knit 6 white sts, k 2 black sts tog, k 9 black sts. <u>Row 14</u>: K 8 black sts, k 2 black sts tog, k 6 white sts, k 2 black sts tog, knit 8 black sts.
Cut black yarn. <u>Rows 15 to 25:</u> Knit white yarn in stockinette.
<u>Rows 25 and 26:</u> Rib K1, P1. Bind off in ribbing.

Strap   Size E crochet hook. Crochet a single chain the correct length to go across the top of the shoe. Stitch down at both ends. Sew up sock, shoe and sole with matching yarn. Tuck in all yarn.

Peasant Costume

Size 1, 3 & 6 needles. G & E crochet hooks.
2 ounces green sport yarn, 1 oz each red,
white & black fingering yarn.

**Knit dress on page 6 with green sport yarn
(minus sleeves).** With G crochet hook
and green yarn single crochet 1 row
around both armholes.

Sleeves	Puffed – With white fingering yarn and size 1 needles cast on 32 sts. Rib K1, P1. 4 rows (for cuff). Change to size 3 needle. K 1 st, increase 1 st across row. (63 sts). Knit 3" from cast on. **Underarm** Bind off 6 sts at beg. of next 2 rows. Then decrease 1 st at beg. and end of every row until 37 sts are left. Knit 2 sts tog. across row, ending with knit 1 st (19 sts). Bind off AND knit 2 sts tog. at the same time. **Finish** Sew sleeve carefully around sleeve hole <u>under</u> green crochet row with green yarn.
Bodice	With size 3 needle and red fingering yarn. Cast on 72 sts. Knit stockinette 10 rows. **Underarm** Knit 11sts (right front), bind off 14 sts (underarm), knit 22 sts (back), cast off 14 sts (underarm), knit 11 sts (left front). **Top** On 11 sts (right front) knit 4 rows. Bind off 6 sts, knit 5 sts 30 rows. (shoulder). Bind off. On 22 sts (back) knit 4 rows. Cast off. On 11 sts (left front) knit 4 rows. Knit 5 sts 30 rows (shoulder). Bind off last 6 sts. Sew shoulder straps to back of bodice.
Border	With black fingering yarn and E crochet hook, single crochet 2 rows around entire vest including armholes.
Lacing	With E crochet hook and yellow embroidery thread crochet a 10" long chain. With tapestry needle, thread chain on to black border of vest (see photo).
Neck	With 2 strands of white fingering yarn, crochet 1 row at neck.

STOCKINETTA
Hair page 16

Peasant Costume – continued

APRON (not shown)
White fingering yarn. Size 3 needles.

> Cast on 44 sts. Row 1. K1, P1, across row. Row 2 K purl st, and p knit sts across row *(those 2 rows are the seed st)* . Knit stockinette keeping the 1st and last 3 sts of every row in seed st. 3-1/2" from cast on. Knit 2 sts tog. across row (22 sts). Rib K1 P1 for 3 rows. Bind off in ribbing. **Tie** With E crochet hook, chain 10", continue and single crochet 1 row across top of apron. Continue and chain 10".
> Iron very gently under a slightly damp cloth to prevent curling.

HALF SLIP (not shown)
White fingering yarn Size 3 needles.

> Starting at the bottom of the slip, cast on 100 sts. Knit 5-1/2" *(so slip shows just below the dress)*.
> **Waist** Knit 2 sts tog. across row. Rib K1 P1 3 rows.
> Bind off in ribbing.
> **Edging** With E crochet hook crochet one row around bottom of slip as follows. *Single crochet 3 sts, chain 3 in next st continue from * around bottom of slip.

Note: Underpants – see page 15.

****

HAT   Crochet. G crochet hook. 2 oz. straw colored 4 ply worsted yarn. All single crochet.

> **Crown** Chain 4, join to make a circle. Chain 2.
> <u>Row 1.</u> Crochet 8 sts in center of 4 st circle.
> *Start every new row by completeing circle with a catch stitch and chaining 2 sts to start next row. Continue in same direction.*
> <u>Row 2</u> Crochet 2 sts in every st (16 sts). <u>Row 3</u> Crochet 2 sts in every st (32 sts). <u>Row 4</u> Crochet 2 sts in every st (64 sts).
> <u>Rows 5, 6, 7, 8, 9</u>   Crochet 1 st in every st (64 sts).
> <u>Row 10</u> * Crochet 1 st in next 3 sts, skip 1*. (34 sts)
> **Brim** <u>Row 11</u>, Crochet 2 sts in every st. (68.) <u>Rows 12, 13, 14</u> Crochet 1 st in every st (68 sts). *Brim will curl.*
> Cut yarn and tuck into brim.
> **Hat band** With red yarn, crochet chain 18" long.

Note: Use same pattern for outfit on page 13. Basic hat white. (Rows 9 & 10 red for hat band, row 14 blue for edge of brim).

Peasant Costume – continued

PULL ON CLOGS
Knit with 2 strands of yarn. Size 5 needles.

Sole with gray yarn. Cast on 20 sts.
Row 1: Knit. Row 2: K 2, inc 1,
k 1, inc 1, k 6, (inc1, k 1) 3 times, inc 1, k 5,
inc 1, k 1, inc 1, k 2, (28 sts on needle).
Row 3: K 10, inc 1, k 3, inc 1,k 2, inc 1, k 3,
inc 1, k 10 (32 sts on needle). Row 4 : K.
Shoe   Change to black yarn.
Row 5: Knit. Row 6: k purl-side row outside
Rows 7-9: Knit 3 rows, *ending with purl row*.
Row 10: K 11, dec 1, k 6, dec 1, k 11, (30 sts).
Row 11: K 10, dec 1 , k 6 , dec 1, k 10 , (28 sts).
Row 12: K 9, dec 1, k 6, dec 1, k 9 (26 sts.)
Row 13: K 8. dec 1, k 6, dec 1, k 8 (24 sts).
Row 14: Rib 1 row. Bind off in ribbing.
With tapestry needle, sew up back and bottom.
Trim with red button on front.

* * * * * * * * * *

STOCKINGS with Tassels.
Unusual flat (not circular) pattern. DIFFICULT
Size 0 and 1 needles 2 oz White fingering yarn,
2 yards of red for tassel. Stockinette

Starting at top of stocking with Size 0 needles, cast on 36 sts.
Rib K 2, p 1 for 8 rows. Change to size 1 needles.
Knit 3" from cast on. Put first and last 9 sts on holder
(to be woven on to the back of the heel 18 sts).
Top of foot Knit center 18 sts 1-1/2" (18 rows).
Toe Knit across row and * hold last st of every row on same needle (do not knit that last st), turn, slip 1, purl back, hold last st, (do not knit), turn, slip 1, continue from * until there are 6 sts left, in center *(and 6 held sts on each end of needle)*.
THEN knit across row and knit <u>one</u> stitch on 'waiting needle' at end of every row until all 18 sts are back on the needle.
Bottom of sock (sole) Knit 18 rows.
Heel Knit (to turn) same as pattern for toe*.

Finish   Weave 18 heel sts onto both 9 sts and 9 sts (18 sts) waiting on holders at back of ankle. Sew up back seam with flat seam stitch. Knit 2nd sock.

Tassel   Wrap red yarn around cardboard 1-1/2" wide. Tie wrapped yarn at one end while on cardboard. Cut yarn at other end. Wrap yarn around tied end tightly. Leave 2" of yarn to sew tassel to stocking.

Cardigan

Size 3 and 6 Needles. 2 oz Sport Yarn
5 small buttons Stockinette.

Back Size 3 needles cast on 40 sts. Rib K1 P1 3 rows. Change to Size 6 needles. Knit stockinette 3" from cast on end with purl row.
Underarm Bind off 5 sts at beg. of next 2 rows. Knit 2".
Shoulders Knit first 5 sts, 5 rows. Bind off. Put center 20 sts on holder (for neck rib). Knit last 5 sts 3 rows. Bind off.

Right Front (Button side) With Size 3 needle cast on 18 sts. Rib 3 rows. Change to size 6 needles. Knit 3" from cast on. End with purl row.
Underarm Bind off 5 sts. Knit 13 sts 2" end with purl row.
Shoulder Knit 5 sts 4 rows. Put 8 sts on holder (for neck rib).

Left Front With size 3 needles cast on 18 sts. Rib 4 rows. Change to size 6 needles. Knit 3", end with knit row.
Underarm Bind off 5 sts. Knit 13 sts 2", end with knit row.
Shoulder Knit 5 sts, 5 rows. Put 8 sts on holder (for neck rib).
Sew back and front shoulders together and sew side seams.

Front Bands (2) Garter Stitch Size 6 needles. First band: Cast on 4 sts, knit 3". Put on holder to be joined to neck rib. Second band: Button hole side. Cast on 4 sts. Knit 3 rows, make first button hole*. Knit button holes every 8th row. (5 button holes with last button hole in 2nd row of neck rib.)
*How to knit button hole row Knit 1 st, yarn over needle ('yarn over' st IS the button hole) knit 2 sts together, knit 1. Next row knit 4 sts. Sew bands on to front of cardigan with flat stitch. *(See page 16)*. *Sew button hole band so that the holes are nearest the sewn seam.*

Neck With Size 3 needles pick up 58 sts as follows: 4 sts of garter st band, 8 sts front, 7 sts one shoulder, 20 sts back, 7 sts other shoulder, 8 sts other front, 4 sts garter st band. Knit both bands in garter st. and the rest of the neck in ribbing of K1, P1 a total of 4 rows. Put last button hole in neck garter st. Bind off.

KNITTY
Hair page 16

Cardigan continued

Sleeves With Size 3 needles cast on 28 sts. Rib K1, P1 4 rows.
Change to Size 6 needles and stockinette.
Knit and increase 4 sts across row evenly (32 sts).
Knit 3-1/2" from cast on.
Underarm Bind off 5 sts at beginning of next 2 rows.
Decrease 1 st at beginning of every knit row until 14 sts are left.
Bind off 3 sts at beginning of next 2 rows.
Bind off last 8 sts.

Finish With tapestry needle sew sleeves into cardigan, starting at underarms.
Sew sleeve seams. Tuck in all loose yarn.
Sew buttons opposite button holes.

* * * * * * * * * * * * * * * * *

PANTS
Knit in 2 pieces. Size 3 & 6 needles. 2 oz sport yarn. Stockinette.

PANTS, right side Size 3 needles, Cast on 26 sts. Rib K1, P1, 4 rows.
Change to size 6 needles. Knit 1 row.
<u>Knit 6 rows at one end for extra inch at back of overalls as follows:</u>
*Knit 6 sts, turn, slip 1 st , k 5 sts. Turn, k 12 sts , turn, slip 1 st ,
k 11 sts. Turn, k 18 sts, turn, slip 1 st, k 17 sts. Turn, knit 26 sts.
**Knit 1 sts and increase 1 st at the beg. of every row until there
are 46 sts.** *(See Note below)*.
(Crotch).
Leg Knit and decrease 1 st both sides every 6th row 3 times. (40 sts).
Knit to 7" from cast on. (2" for shorts). Change to size 3 needles.
Rib K 1, P 1 3 rows. Bind off in ribbing.

LEFT SIDE OF PANTS Size 3 needles. Cast on 26 sts. Rib K1, P 1, 4 rows.
Change to size 6 needles and knit 2 rows.
Knit from *. After knitting the 6 back rows **STOP** and check that
the rows on both knitted parts are on the correct (opposite) side from
each other where both pieces will join, *for that extra inch at the back*.
Continue with pattern above.

Finish With flat stitch *(see page 16)* join 2 pieces from cast on to crotch,
on both sides. *(Back seam is longer than front)*. Sew both leg seams
from crotch to ankle.

Note: To increase or decrease sts <u>always make or remove the second stitch
IN from the edge</u>. (i.e. K 1,increase 1 or k 1, dec. 1.) To **increase**
for a neat hidden st, pick up new stitch <u>from the back</u> of the next knit
stitch <u>one row down</u>.

Easy (to knit) Undies
Size 3 needles White Fingering Yarn.
Stockinette.   Underpants for peasant costume.

Waist   Cast on 80 sts. Knit 2 rows.
Row 3. *Knit 1, Knit 2 sts tog, yarn over – repeat from *
(for draw string waist band). Knit 4".

Divide for legs
Put 2 sts on holder, knit 36 sts, put 4 sts on holder, knit 36 sts,
put last 2 sts on holder.
Knit 36 sts 1". Bind off. Knit other leg 36 sts 1". Bind off.

Finish   Sew back seam. Sew neatly (*or weave – see page 16*)
4 back sts to 4 front sts for crotch. Sew leg seams.

SNEAKERS (2)
1 oz blue sport yarn. 1/2 oz white. Stockinette.
Size 5 needles. Knit with two strands of yarn.

Sole   Two strands of white yarn
Cast on 20 sts.
<u>Row 1</u> Knit
<u>Row 2</u> Purl 2 sts, inc 1 st, k1 st, inc 1 st, purl 6 sts, (inc 1 st, purl 1 st)
3 times, inc 1 st, purl 5 sts, inc 1 st, purl 1 st, inc 1 st, purl 2 sts
(28 sts on needle).
<u>Row 3</u> Knit 10 sts, inc 1 st, knit 3 sts, inc 1 st, knit 2 sts, inc 1 st,
knit 3 sts, inc 1 st, knit 10 sts (32 sts on needle).
Shoe, change to 2 strands blue yarn.
Row 4 K
Row 5 Knit purl-side out (for shoe ridge).
Knit 6 Knit
Row 7 Purl
Row 8 Knit
Row 9 Purl 11 sts, purl 2 sts tog, purl 6 sts, purl 2 sts tog.
purl 11 sts (30 sts)
Row 10 Knit 10 sts, k 2 sts tog, knit 6 sts, k 2 sts tog, knit 10 sts, (28 sts).
Row 11 Purl 9 sts, purl 2 sts tog, purl 6 sts, purl 2 sts tog,
purl 9 sts (26 sts).
Row 12 Knit 8 sts, k 2 sts tog, k 6 sts, k 2 sts tog, k 8 sts (24 sts).
Bind off, purling, with white yarn.

With tapestry needle, sew up back and bottom.
With single strand stitch a white x and make a bow on front of sneaker.

Hair Styles

Yarn for hair can be attached to the dolls head that is knit with skin color or can be added to a hair color yarn already knit on the head (as with the dolls in this book). Yarn for hair can be all kinds of textures; cotton, wool, silk etc. For an original touch all kinds of colors can be used as well. Acrylic yarn is the sturdiest.

Purlie's CURLS Directions on page 4.

Stockinetta's BRAIDS page 10. Cut 32 strands about 20" long. Fold two strands of yarn evenly into each stitch on the first row of hair around the hair line, except for the front section over the face. Separate yarn into two bunches. Braid one bunch for each side of head. For a 'ribbon' on braids, crochet a chain the same color yarn as outfit about 6" long. Tie firmly one inch from the end of braids.
FRONT BANGS For a little fringe above Stockinetta's face, cut eight 8" strands of yarn in hair color. With tapestry needle stitch each strand of yarn <u>two times</u> into each stitch on the first row of hair color yarn firmly, so that it does not slip out (that extra twist in stitching should hold the yarn in place). Make sure the yarn <u>hangs down</u> over the top of the face. Trim bangs.

Knitty's Sleek, Chic and Easy page 13. Follow the pattern on page 3 and leave it as is, without any more fuss.

****

KNITTING TIPS

Stockinette – <u>Knit One Row, Purl One Row.</u>

Garter Stitch – <u>Knit Every Row.</u>

Ribbing – <u>Knit One Stitch, Purl One Stitch.</u>

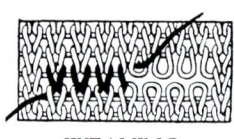
WEAVING STITCH

DUPLICATE STITCH

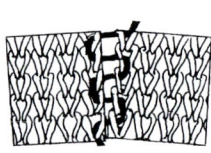
FLAT SEAM STOCKINETTE

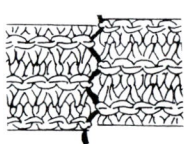
FLAT SEAM GARTER STITCH